We Were Dancing

**A Comedy in Two Scenes
from**
Tonight at 8:30

by Noël Coward

A Samuel French Acting Edition

SAMUELFRENCH.COM

Copyright © 1936, 1938, 1963, 1965 by Noël Coward

ALL RIGHTS RESERVED

CAUTION: Professionals and amateurs are hereby warned that *WE WERE DANCING* is subject to a Licensing Fee. It is fully protected under the copyright laws of the United States of America, the British Commonwealth, including Canada, and all other countries of the Copyright Union. All rights, including professional, amateur, motion picture, recitation, lecturing, public reading, radio broadcasting, television and the rights of translation into foreign languages are strictly reserved. In its present form the play is dedicated to the reading public only.

The amateur live stage performance rights to *WE WERE DANCING* are controlled exclusively by Samuel French, Inc., and licensing arrangements and performance licenses must be secured well in advance of presentation. PLEASE NOTE that amateur Licensing Fees are set upon application in accordance with your producing circumstances. When applying for a licensing quotation and a performance license please give us the number of performances intended, dates of production, your seating capacity and admission fee. Licensing Fees are payable one week before the opening performance of the play to Samuel French, Inc., at 45 W. 25th Street, New York, NY 10010.

Licensing Fee of the required amount must be paid whether the play is presented for charity or gain and whether or not admission is charged.

Stock licensing fees quoted upon application to Samuel French, Inc.

For all other rights than those stipulated above, apply to: Samuel French, Inc., at 45 W. 25th Street, New York, NY 10010.

Particular emphasis is laid on the question of amateur or professional readings, permission and terms for which must be secured in writing from Samuel French, Inc.

Copying from this book in whole or in part is strictly forbidden by law, and the right of performance is not transferable.

Whenever the play is produced the following notice must appear on all programs, printing and advertising for the play: "Produced by special arrangement with Samuel French, Inc."

Due authorship credit must be given on all programs, printing and advertising for the play.

No one shall commit or authorize any act or omission by which the copyright of, or the right to copyright, this play may be impaired.
No one shall make any changes in this play for the purpose of production.
Publication of this play does not imply availability for performance. Both amateurs and professionals considering a production are strongly advised in their own interests to apply to Samuel French, Inc., for written permission before starting rehearsals, advertising, or booking a theatre.
No part of this book may be reproduced, stored in a retrieval system, or transmitted in any form, by any means, now known or yet to be invented, including mechanical, electronic, photocopying, recording, videotaping, or otherwise, without the prior written permission of the publisher.

ISBN 978-0-573-62578-7   Printed in U.S.A.   #25627

WE WERE DANCING

Produced by John C. Wilson at the National Theatre in New York City on November 27, 1936, as one of a series of nine one-act plays by Noel Coward, under the title of "TO-NIGHT AT EIGHT-THIRTY." The play was directed by the author and the cast was as follows:

KARL SANDYS	*Noel Coward.*
LOUISE CHARTERIS	*Gertrude Lawrence.*
IPPAGA	*Kenneth Carten.*
GEORGE DAVIES	*Edward Underdown.*
EVA BLAKE	*Moya Nugent.*
CLARA BETHEL	*Joyce Carey.*
HUBERT CHARTERIS . . .	*Alan Webb.*
MAJOR BLAKE	*Anthony Pelissier.*

Two or three unnamed members of the Country Club.

SCENE I.—Verandah of the Country Club at Samolo. Evening.

SCENE II.—The same. Early morning.

TIME.—The Present.

WE WERE DANCING

Produced at the Phœnix Theatre, Charing Cross Road, London, W.C.2, in January, 1936, with the following cast of Characters:

CHARACTERS

LOUISE CHARTERIS	*Gertrude Lawrence.*
HUBERT CHARTERIS	*Alan Webb.*
KARL SANDYS	*Noel Coward.*
CLARA BETHEL	*Alison Leggatt.*
GEORGE DAVIES	*Edward Underdown.*
EVA BLAKE	*Moya Nugent.*
MAJOR BLAKE	*Anthony Pelissier.*
IPPAGA	*Kenneth Carten.*

Two or three unnamed members of the Country Club.

SCENE I.—Verandah of the Country Club at Samolo. Evening.
SCENE II.—The same. Early morning.

TIME.—The Present.

WE WERE DANCING

The SCENE is the verandah of the Country Club at Samolo. On the R. is a room in which dances are held every Saturday night. For these occasions a dance band flies up from Pendarla by the new Imperial Inter-State Airways. The band arrives in the afternoon, plays all night and departs early on Sunday for Abbachi, where it repeats the same procedure for the inhabitants there, returning wearily on Mondays to the Grand Hotel, Pendarla, where, during the week, it plays for the Tourists.

When the CURTAIN rises the verandah is deserted. A full moon is shining over the sea and, far away, above the chatter and music of the dance room, there can occasionally be heard the wailing of native music rising up from the crowded streets by the harbour.

IPPAGA, *a Samolan boy, crosses the verandah from* L. *to* R. *carrying a tray of drinks. He is yellowish brown in colour and, like most Samolans, comparatively tall. He wears a scarlet fez, a green, purple and mustard-coloured sarong, black patent leather shoes, silver earrings and three wooden bracelets. As he goes off on the* R. *the dance music stops and there is the sound of applause.*

GEORGE DAVIES *and* EVA BLAKE *come out of the dance room.* GEORGE DAVIES *is a hearty, nondescript young man dressed in the usual white mess jacket, black evening trousers and cummerbund.* EVA, *equally nondescript, is wearing a pink taffeta bunchy little dress, pink ribbon in her hair, and pink shoes and stockings which do not quite match. She carries a diamond evening bag and a blue chiffon handkerchief round her wrist. She also wears a necklace of seed pearls and a pendant.*

The dance music starts again. EVA *looks furtively over her shoulder.*

GEORGE *enters first and walks up to the balcony, then calls:*

GEORGE. Eva! Eva!

EVA (*entering*). It's all right, they're playing an encore.

GEORGE. Come on, then.

EVA. Where's the car?

GEORGE. I parked it at the end of the garden, where the road turns off. My boy's looking after it.

EVA. He won't say anything, will he?

GEORGE. Of course not. He's been with me for years.

EVA. Oh, George!

GEORGE (*impatiently*). It's all right—come on——

EVA. Where are we going?

GEORGE. Mahica beach, nobody ever comes near it.

EVA. Oh, George!

GEORGE (*taking her hand*). Come on——

(*They go off up* R. IPPAGA *crosses from* R. *to* L. *with a tray on which are two empty glasses.*

The band is playing a waltz and the stage is empty for a moment. LOUISE CHARTERIS *and* KARL SANDYS *come dancing in from the* R. *They are both in the thirties, soignée and well-dressed, and they dance together as though they had never been apart. They waltz three times round the stage, finishing in the centre with a prolonged kiss. The music ends, there is the sound of applause.* TWO WOMEN *and a* MAN *come in. They stop short on observing* LOUISE *and* KARL. *They whisper together for a moment and then go back into the dance room.* LOUISE *and* KARL *remain clasped in each other's arms oblivious of everything.*

The music starts again.

HUBERT CHARTERIS *and* CLARA BETHEL *come out of the dance room.* CLARA *is a nice-looking grey-haired woman in the forties.* HUBERT, *her brother, is about the same age. He has dignity and reserve and looks intelligently British. They both stand for a moment looking at* KARL *and* LOUISE *who, still entranced with their kiss, have not even noticed them.*)

HUBERT (*quietly*). Louise.
LOUISE (*jumping*). Oh!
CLARA (*reproachfully*). Louise, really!

(LOUISE *and* KARL *step a little away from each other.*)

LOUISE (*with a social manner*). This is my husband. (*She hesitates and turns to* KARL.) I'm afraid I didn't catch your name?
KARL. Karl. Karl Sandys. (*To* HUBERT *and* CLARA.) How do you do? (*He makes an abortive movement to shake hands.*)
HUBERT (*with perfect control*). The car's here, I think we'd better go if you're ready.
LOUISE. I'm not ready.
CLARA (*going towards her*). Come along, Louise.
LOUISE. I can't go, really I can't.
HUBERT. This is most embarrassing, please don't make it worse.
LOUISE. I'm sorry, Hubert. I do see that it's all very difficult.
KARL. I fear I was partly to blame.
HUBERT (*ignoring him*). Please come home now, Louise.
LOUISE (*gently*). No, Hubert.
HUBERT. I'm afraid I must insist.
LOUISE. We have fallen in love. (*She takes* KARL'S *hand.*)
KARL. Deeply in love.
HUBERT. I would prefer not to discuss the matter with you, sir.
LOUISE. That's silly, Hubert.
HUBERT (*sternly*). Please come away.
LOUISE. I've told you, I can't.
KARL. Have a drink?
HUBERT (*irritably*). Good God! (*He half turns away.*)

Louise. That is a good idea, Hubert, let's all have a drink.

Karl. We might also sit down.

Clara (*crossing* Hubert *to* Louise). Listen, Louise, you can't behave like this, it's too idiotic.

Louise. It's true, can't you see? It's true.

Clara. What's true? Don't be so foolish.

Karl. We're in love, that's what's true, really it is, Mrs.—Mrs.—— (*He crosses to* Clara c.)

Louise (*moving down* l.). Bethel. This is my husband's sister, Mrs. Bethel.

Karl. How do you do? (*He shakes hands.*)

Clara. I appeal to you, Mr.—Mr.——

Karl. Sandys.

Clara. Mr. Sandys—please go away. Go away at once.

Karl. That's quite impossible.

Hubert (*moving down*). I detest scenes and I am finding this very unpleasant. I don't know who you are or where you come from, but if you have any sense of behaviour at all you must see that this situation is intolerable. Will you kindly leave the club immediately and never speak to my wife again in any circumstances whatever?

Louise (*crossing to* Hubert). It's more important than that, Hubert, really it is.

Karl (*crossing to* Hubert). It's the most important thing that has ever happened to me in my whole life, Mr.—Mr.——

Louise. Charteris.

Karl. Mr. Charteris.

Hubert (*crossing* Karl *to* Louise). Once more, Louise, for the last time, will you come home?

Louise. No—I can't.

Hubert. Very well. Come, Clara.

(*He turns to go away.* Louise *catches his arm.* Clara *moves a little* c.)

Louise. You can't go, either. I know you hate scenes and I'm apparently behaving very badly, but it's true, this thing that's happened I mean—we have fallen in love——

HUBERT. Please let go of my arm, Louise, and don't be ridiculous.

LOUISE. Look at me—look closely—I've been your wife for thirteen years. You're wise and intelligent and you know me well—— Look at me! (*He backs away to* L.)

CLARA (*anxiously*). Please go, Mr. Sandys.

KARL (*shaking his head*). No.

HUBERT (*to* LOUISE). I'm looking at you.

LOUISE (*emotionally*). Well—don't you see ?

(HUBERT *looks quickly at* CLARA, *then at* KARL *and then back to* LOUISE *again.*)

HUBERT. Yes—I see. (*He takes a step down to her, then looks at* CLARA. *He then takes another step down to look up at* KARL; *then he goes up stage.*)

CLARA. Hubert.

(MAJOR BLAKE *comes in from the dance room. He is a red-faced elderly man.*)

MAJOR BLAKE. I say, has anybody seen Eva ?

HUBERT. What ?

MAJOR BLAKE. I can't find Eva.

CLARA (*between* KARL *and* LOUISE). I think she went home.

MAJOR BLAKE. She can't have, the car's still there.

CLARA. She told me she was driving back with the Baileys.

MAJOR BLAKE. Oh, did she, did she really ?

CLARA. She told practically everybody in the club that she was driving back with the Baileys, I'm surprised she didn't mention it to you.

MAJOR BLAKE. Oh, she's all right, then—thanks—thanks awfully.

CLARA (*after a pause*). You'll be able to pick her up on the way home.

MAJOR BLAKE. It's hardly on the way, it means going all round by the Woo Ching road.

HUBERT. Why not telephone her?

MAJOR BLAKE. They won't have got there yet, it's an hour's drive.

CLARA. Why not wait until she has got there?

MAJOR BLAKE. Yes, I suppose I'd better. Anybody feel like a Stengah?

HUBERT. No, thanks.

MAJOR BLAKE (*to* KARL). Do you, sir?

KARL. No, thank you.

MAJOR BLAKE. All right—I shall go into the bar——

KARL. Bar!

MAJOR BLAKE. Thanks very much.

(*He crosses below all but* LOUISE *and goes out* L. LOUISE *turns her head as he gets to the entrance and watches him out.*)

KARL. Who is Eva?

(HUBERT *walks up to the balcony.*)

CLARA. His wife.

KARL. And who are the Baileys?

CLARA (*with irritation*). Does it matter?

KARL. I don't know.

LOUISE. They live in that large reddish-looking house at the top of the hill.

KARL. I've never been to the top of the hill.

CLARA. Good night, Mr. Sandys. (*She crosses to him and shakes his outstretched hand.*)

KARL. Good night.

CLARA (*with almost overdone ordinariness, crossing to* LOUISE). Come along, Louise.

LOUISE. Don't be silly, Clara.

CLARA. I'm not being silly. I'm acutely uncomfortable. You're behaving abominably and putting Hubert in an insufferable position. For heaven's sake, pull yourself together and be reasonable. You talk a lot of nonsense about being in love. How could you have possibly fallen in love all in a minute like that——

KARL. We have.

CLARA. Please be quiet and let me speak.

LOUISE. Hubert, do make Clara shut up.
CLARA. You must be insane.
HUBERT. Shut up, Clara. (*He moves to* CLARA *and up again.*)
CLARA. And you must be insane too, I'm ashamed of you, Hubert.
LOUISE (*moving up to* CLARA). It's no use railing and roaring, Clara. Hubert's much wiser than you. He's keeping calm and trying to understand and I'm deeply grateful to him——
CLARA. Grateful indeed!
LOUISE. Yes, if he behaved as you seem to think he ought to behave, it would only make everything far worse. I suppose you want him to knock Mr.—— (*To* KARL.) What is your first name?
KARL. Karl.
LOUISE. Karl in the jaw. (*She walks up* L.)

(*They all turn away from her.*)

CLARA. I don't want anything of the sort. I want him to treat the situation as it should be treated, as nothing but a joke, a stupid joke in extremely bad taste. (*She sits* R. *of the* L. *table.*)
LOUISE. It's more than that, Clara, and you know it is, that's why you're scared.
CLARA. I'm not in the least scared.
HUBERT (*coming down to* CLARA). You'd better allow me to deal with this, Clara, in my own way.
CLARA. There is such a thing as being too wise, too understanding.
LOUISE. You're usually pretty intelligent yourself, Clara. I can't think what's happened to you. This thing is here—now—between Karl and me. It's no use pretending it isn't, or trying to flip it away as a joke, nor is it any use taking up a belligerent attitude over it. (*Moving up and down.*) God knows I'm confused enough myself—utterly bewildered, but I do know that it's real, too real to be dissipated by conventional gestures——
CLARA. What is real? What are you talking about?

KARL. Love, Mrs. Bethel, we've fallen in love.

CLARA. Rubbish!

LOUISE. It's not rubbish! Be quiet!

HUBERT (*to* LOUISE—*coming down* L.). What do you want me to do?

LOUISE (*looking at* KARL). I don't know.

KARL (*crossing to* HUBERT). May I ask you a question?

HUBERT (*stiffly*). What is it?

KARL. Are you in love with Louise?

(CLARA *rises.*)

CLARA. Well, really!

HUBERT. I am devoted to Louise. We have been married for many years.

KARL. I said are you in love with her?

HUBERT. I love her.

LOUISE. Don't go on evading, Hubert, you know perfectly well what he means.

HUBERT. Of course I know what he means. (*To* KARL.) I'll answer you truly. I am not in love with Louise in the way that you imagine yourself to be in love with her——

KARL (*looking at* LOUISE). I worship her.

HUBERT. You know nothing about her.

KARL. I know that suddenly, when we were dancing, an enchantment swept over me. An enchantment that I have never known before and shall never know again. It's obvious that you should think I'm mad and that she's mad too, our behaviour looks idiotic, cheap, anything you like, but it's true, this magic that happened, it's so true that everything else, all the ordinary ways of behaviour look shabby and unreal beside it—my heart's thumping, I'm trembling like a fool, even now when I'm trying so hard, so desperately hard to be calm and explain to you reasonably, I daren't look at her, if I did, my eyes would brim over with these silly tears and I should cry like a child——

LOUISE (*making a movement towards him*). Oh, my darling——

KARL (*moving up to the balcony*). Don't, don't speak —let him speak, let him say what's to be done.

(HUBERT *drops down* L. KARL *leaves the three of them and goes up to the verandah-rail and looks out at the sea.*)

CLARA. You didn't even know his name.
LOUISE. Oh, Clara! What the hell does that matter?
CLARA (*crossing to* LOUISE). This is really too fantastic—it's beyond belief—it's——

LOUISE (*gently, to* CLARA *by her*). Listen—I know you feel dreadfully upset for Hubert, and for me too, but it's no use huffing and puffing and getting yourself into a state. Here it is, this thing that's happened—as large as life—larger than life and we'd all better look at it clearly and as sensibly as we can.

(HUBERT *paces* L. *and* R. KARL *sits* L. *of the* R. *table;* CLARA R. *of the* L. *table.*)

HUBERT. You go home, Clara, you can send the car back for me.
CLARA. I shall do no such thing.

(HUBERT *moves away* R. *and back* C.)

LOUISE (*hurriedly to* HUBERT). We'd better go away —he and I—as soon as possible.
HUBERT. Where to?
LOUISE. I don't know—anywhere——
HUBERT. For God's sake, be reasonable. How can you? How can I let you?
LOUISE. How much do you mind—really?
HUBERT. That obviously has nothing to do with it.
LOUISE. I want to know.
HUBERT. I want to know too. I can't possibly tell. You've made this up, this magic that he talked about, you've conjured it out of the air and now it's smeared over everything—over me too—none of it seems real, but it has to be treated as if it were. You ask me how

much I mind—you want that as well, don't you, in addition to your new love?

LOUISE. Want what! What do you mean?

HUBERT (*almost losing control*). You want me to mind—don't you—don't you?

LOUISE. Oh, Hubert—please don't look like that——

HUBERT. You want everything—everything in the world, you always have.

LOUISE. You're pitying yourself. How beastly of you to be so weak, how contemptible of you!

CLARA. Louise! (*She rises and comes down.*)

(KARL *rises too.*)

LOUISE. I've been faithful to you all these years. We stopped being in love with each other ages ago——we became a habit—a well-ordered, useful, social habit. Have you been as faithful to me as I have to you?

KARL (*coming down* C.). That's nothing to do with us—what's the use of arguing? (*He joins the group again.*)

LOUISE. Answer me. Have you?

HUBERT. No.

CLARA. Hubert!

LOUISE. Fair's fair.

CLARA. Hubert! Louise!

LOUISE. Do stop saying, Hubert and Louise, Clara, (*with her back to the audience*) it's maddening.

(KARL *comes down between* CLARA *and* HUBERT. LOUISE *has her back to the audience still.*)

KARL. What is all this? Can't you keep to the point both of you? What does it matter whether he's been faithful to you or not, or you to him either? You're not in love with each other any more, that's clear enough, and even if you were, this forked lightning that has struck Louise and me would shatter it—scorch it out of existence——

CLARA. Forked lightning indeed!

KARL (*going up stage*). Earthquake then, tidal wave, cataclysm!

HUBERT (*going to* LOUISE). I've never not loved you, Louise.

LOUISE (*irritably*). I know. I'm deeply attached to you, too. I hated it when you had your tiresome little affairs on the side——

HUBERT. With your heart?

LOUISE. Of course not. Don't be so damned sentimental. You haven't come near my heart for years. (*She turns to* CLARA.)

CLARA. If Hubert doesn't strike you in a minute, I will.

(LOUISE *moves up stage.* IPPAGA *comes out of the dance room with an empty tray.*)

KARL. Boy, bring four whisky and sodas.

IPPAGA. Yes, sir.

LOUISE. They're called Stengahs here.

KARL. Four Stengahs, then.

CLARA. I'd rather have lemonade. (*She drops down* R.)

KARL. You seem bent on complicating everything. (*To* IPPAGA.) Four Stengahs.

IPPAGA. Yes, sir.

(IPPAGA *goes off.*)

LOUISE. Karl, where were we?

HUBERT. Nowhere—nowhere at all. (*He turns away.*)

KARL (*to* HUBERT). Listen, Charteris—I know you won't believe me, or even care, but I really am dreadfully sorry about all this—not about falling in love, that's beyond being sorry about, but that it should happen to be your wife——

HUBERT. Who are you, where do you come from?

KARL. My name is Karl Sandys. I come from Hampshire. My father is Admiral Sandys——

LOUISE. Dear darling, I wouldn't mind if he were only a bosun's mate. (*She moves down.*)

KARL. I know you wouldn't, but I must explain to your husband——

CLARA. How you can have the impertinence to be flippant, Louise, at a moment like this——

KARL. Perhaps you would like a cigarette. (*Offering* HUBERT *one.*)

LOUISE. There's never been a moment like this, never before in the history of the world—I'm delirious.

HUBERT (*to* KARL). Please go on.

KARL. I was in the Navy myself, but I was axed in nineteen-twenty-four.

LOUISE. What's axed?

KARL. Kicked out.

LOUISE. Oh dear, whatever for?

HUBERT. Never mind that, I understand, go on.

KARL. I'm now in the shipping business. I represent the I.M.C.L.

LOUISE. What in God's name is the I.M.C.L.?

HUBERT. Imperial Malayan China Line.

KARL. Passenger and Freight.

HUBERT. I know.

KARL. I've come from Singapore, I've been interviewing our agents in Pendarla——

HUBERT. Littlejohn Thurston and Company.

KARL. Yes. Littlejohn Thurston and Company.

LOUISE (*to* CLARA). Littlejohn Thurston and Company.

KARL. I flew up here in the morning 'plane because I wanted to see a little of the country before I sail on Wednesday.

LOUISE. On Wednesday!

HUBERT. Are you married?

KARL. I was, but we were divorced in nineteen-twenty-seven.

LOUISE. Oh, Karl. Did you love her? (*She goes to him.*)

KARL. Of course I did.

LOUISE. The moment's changed—I'm not delirious any more—I can't think of you ever having loved anybody but me—— (*She moves up.*)

HUBERT. Have you any money?

KARL. Not very much—enough. (*He moves after her and turns.*)

LOUISE. What was her name?

KARL. Ayleen.

LOUISE. You mean Eileen.

KARL. I do not, I mean Ayleen—A-y-l-e-e-n.

LOUISE. Very affected. (*She moves down* L.)

KARL (*crossing to* LOUISE). It's you I love, more than anyone in the world, past or future——

LOUISE. Oh, Karl!

(*They embrace.*)

HUBERT (*sharply*). Please—just a moment—both of you.

KARL. I'm sorry. (*To* HUBERT.) That was inconsiderate.

HUBERT. I'm trying to be as detached as possible. It isn't easy.

LOUISE. I know it isn't, it's beastly for you, I do see that.

CLARA. You're all being so charming to each other it's positively nauseating.

LOUISE. My dear Clara, just because your late husband was vaguely connected with the Indian Army, there is no reason for you to be so set on blood-letting——

(KARL *puts his cigarette out at* L. *table.*)

CLARA. I'm not—I should like to say——

LOUISE. You're no better than a Tricoteuse.

KARL. What's a Tricoteuse?

LOUISE. One of those horrid old things in the French Revolution with knitting-needles.

HUBERT. All this is beside the point.

LOUISE. Clara's been beside the point for years.

KARL. Dearest, I want you so.

(*They embrace.*)

LOUISE. Oh, Karl!

CLARA. This is disgusting——

HUBERT. You'd much better go home, Clara——

CLARA. I've told you before I shall do no such thing, I'm apparently the only one present with the remotest grip on sanity. I shall stay as long as you do, Hubert.

KARL. Dear Mrs. Bethel.

CLARA. I beg your pardon?

KARL (*crossing to* CLARA). I said " Dear Mrs. Bethel " because I admire your integrity enormously and I do hope when all this has blown over that we shall be close friends.

CLARA. I think you're an insufferable cad, Mr. Sandys.

LOUISE. Blown over! Oh, Karl!

KARL. Darling, I didn't mean that part of it.

HUBERT. I have something to say to you, Louise. Will everybody please be quiet for a moment?

CLARA. Hubert, I honestly think——

LOUISE. That's exactly what you don't do.

HUBERT. This man, whom you so abruptly love, is sailing on Wednesday.

KARL. On the *Euripides*.

LOUISE. But the *Euripides* goes to Australia, I know because the MacVities are going on it.

KARL. That can't be helped, I have to interview our agents in Sydney——

LOUISE. We'll have to go on another boat, I can't travel in sin with the MacVities.

HUBERT. Do you really mean to go with him?

LOUISE. Yes, Hubert.

CLARA. You're stark staring mad all of you; Hubert, for God's sake——

HUBERT. Excuse me. (*Gently.*) Louise, how true is this to you?

LOUISE. Oh, Hubert, don't be too kind.

HUBERT. Will it be worth it?

LOUISE. Oh yes, yes, of course it will—it must.

HUBERT. What has happened exactly—how do you know so surely, so soon?

Song: "We Were Dancing."

Verse 1.

If you can
Imagine my embarrassment when you politely asked me
    to explain
Man to man,
I cannot help but feel conventional apologies are all in
    vain.
You must see
We've stepped into a dream that's set us free;
Don't think we planned it,
Please understand it.

Refrain.

We were dancing
And the Gods must have found it entrancing
For they smiled
On a moment undefiled
By the care and woe
That mortals know.
We were dancing
And the music and lights were enhancing
Our desire—
When the World caught on fire.
He and I were dancing.

Verse 2.

Love lay in wait for us,
Twisted our fate for us,
No one warned us,
Reason scorned us,
Time stood still
In that first strange thrill.
Destiny knew of us,
Guided the two of us,
How could we
Refuse to see

That wrong seemed right
On this lyrical enchanted night;
Logic supplies no laws for it
Only one cause for it.

We were dancing, etc. . . . (*Repeat refrain.*)

LOUISE. We were dancing—somebody introduced us, I can't remember who, we never heard each other's names—it was a waltz—and in the middle of it we looked at each other—he said just now that it was forked lightning, an earthquake, a tidal wave, a cataclysm, but it was more than all those things—much more—my heart stopped, and with it the world stopped too—there was no more land or sea or sky, there wasn't even any more music—I saw in his eyes a strange infinity—only just him and me together for ever and ever—and—ever——

(*She faints.* KARL *catches her in his arms.* IPPAGA *enters* L. *with a tray of drinks.*)

IPPAGA. Stengahs, sir.
KARL. Bring them here, quick.

(KARL *lowers* LOUISE *gently into a chair and kneels beside her with his arm under her head.* HUBERT *kneels on the other side of her.* CLARA *kneels in front of her and endeavours to make her swallow a little whisky. After a moment her eyelids flutter and she moves her head.*

The dance music which has been playing intermittently throughout the scene comes to an end, there is the sound of applause, then it strikes up the National Anthem.)

LOUISE (*weakly*). Good God! God save the King!

(*She staggers to her feet, supported by* KARL. *The others rise also and they all stand to attention as the lights fade on the scene.*)

SCENE II

When the lights come up on the Scene, CLARA, HUBERT, LOUISE *and* KARL *are all sitting in attitudes of extreme weariness. On the* L. *table are the remains of bacon and eggs and sandwiches.* IPPAGA *is lying on the floor on the* R., *fast asleep. Dawn is breaking and the stage gets lighter and lighter as the scene progresses.* LOUISE, *in a state of drooping exhaustion, is arranging her face in the mirror from her hand-bag which* HUBERT *is holding up for her.*

LOUISE (*petulantly*). . . . But surely you could interview your agents in Sydney another time——

KARL. I can't see why I should alter the whole course of my career just because of the MacVities.

LOUISE. It isn't only the MacVities, it's Australia.

KARL. What's the matter with Australia?

LOUISE. I don't know, that's what's worrying me.

HUBERT. Haven't you got any agents anywhere else?

KARL. There's Havermeyer, Turner and Price in Johannesburg, but I've seen them.

LOUISE. You could see them again, couldn't you? It's not much to ask.

KARL. If I start giving in to you now, darling, we shall never have a moment's peace together.

CLARA. Well, I wish you'd make up your minds where you're going and when, it's very early and I'm tired.

LOUISE. You've both been wonderful—I'm tired too.

HUBERT. Would you like another sandwich, dear? There are three left.

LOUISE (*patting his hand*). No, thank you, Hubert, they're filthy.

KARL. I'd like to say too how grateful I am to you; you've been understanding and direct and absolutely first-rate over the whole business.

HUBERT. I'm terribly fond of Louise, I always have been.

CLARA. Fortunately Hubert's leave is almost due,

so we shan't have to face too much unpleasantness in the Colony.

HUBERT. What time does your 'plane leave?

KARL (*glancing at his watch*). Seven-thirty—it's now a quarter to six.

LOUISE. I'll come by the night train and join you in Pendarla in the morning.

HUBERT. I shall miss you dreadfully, Louise.

LOUISE. I shall miss you too.

KARL. I am not sure that I shan't miss you too.

LOUISE. Oh dear, I do wish it didn't have to be Australia.

KARL. Now then, Louise!

CLARA. Some parts of Australia can be lovely.

LOUISE. Yes, Clara, but will they?

CLARA. And there's always New Zealand.

KARL. I haven't any agents in New Zealand.

LOUISE. I shall have to write to mother and explain. I'm afraid it will be dreadfully muddling for her.

HUBERT. Serve her right.

LOUISE. Hubert! It's not like you to be unchivalrous about mother.

HUBERT. Now that you are leaving me the situation has changed.

LOUISE. Yes, of course I do see that.

HUBERT. Without wishing to wound you, Louise, I should like to take this opportunity of saying that your mother lacks charm to a remarkable degree.

LOUISE. It's funny, isn't it, when you think how attractive father was.

KARL. This seems an ideal moment for you to give us a detailed description of where you lived as a girl.

LOUISE. I do hope you're not going to turn out to be testy.

(CLARA, HUBERT *and* KARL *rise*.)

CLARA. Well, never mind, come along, Hubert, we can't stay here any longer, the Fenwicks will be arriving to play golf in a minute.

(KARL *goes over* L.)

HUBERT (*to* LOUISE). Do you want to come now or stay until his 'plane goes?

LOUISE. I'll stay just for a little while; you can send the car back.

HUBERT (*to* KARL). Would you care to come to the house and have a bath? (*He crosses to* KARL.)

KARL. No, thanks, I can have one here.

HUBERT. Then I shan't be seeing you again.

KARL. Not unless you come and see us off on the boat.

HUBERT. I shan't be able to on Wednesday, I have to go up country.

KARL. Well, good-bye, then.

HUBERT. Good-bye.

(*They shake hands.*)

Try to make her happy, won't you?

KARL. I'll do my best.

HUBERT. Clara——

CLARA (*to* KARL). Good-bye. (*She is near* R. *entrance.*)

KARL. Good-bye.

CLARA. I wish my husband were alive. Because he'd horsewhip you and, Tricoteuse or no Tricoteuse, I should enjoy it keenly.

(CLARA *and* HUBERT *go off up* R. LOUISE *gets up and goes to the verandah-rail; she leans on it and looks out at the sea.*)

LOUISE. I feel as if I'd been run over.

KARL (*joining her*). Dearest.

LOUISE. Don't.

KARL. Don't what?

LOUISE. Don't call me dearest, just for a minute.

KARL. I love you so.

LOUISE. We ought to be able to see Sumatra really at this time of the morning.

KARL. I don't want to see Sumatra.

LOUISE. I think I will have another sandwich after all. (*She offers him one, which he takes.*)

KARL. All right.

(*They come down stage.*)

LOUISE. Are you happy?
KARL. Wildly happy. Are you?
LOUISE. Dear Karl.
KARL. What's the matter?
LOUISE. You're doing splendidly.
KARL. Don't talk like that, it's unkind.
LOUISE. Ayleen would be proud of you.
KARL. That was worse than unkind.
LOUISE. Where is it, our moment? What's happened to the magic?
KARL (*sadly*). I see.
LOUISE. I wonder if you do really.
KARL (*throwing away his sandwich*). Dance with me a minute.
LOUISE. Very well.

(*She hasn't quite finished her sandwich, so she holds it in her left hand while they waltz solemnly round the stage.*)

KARL. Of course the music makes a great difference.
LOUISE. There isn't always music.
KARL. And moonlight.
LOUISE. Moonlight doesn't last.

(*They go on dancing. The sound of a native pipe is heard a long way off in the distance.*)

KARL. There's music for us.
LOUISE. It's the wrong sort.
KARL. I wish you'd finish your sandwich.
LOUISE. I have.
KARL. Kiss me.
LOUISE. My dear——

(*They kiss.*)

You see!
KARL. The joke is on us. (*He moves away a little.*)
LOUISE. It was a nice joke, while it lasted.
KARL. We've never even been lovers.
LOUISE. I don't want to now, do you?

KARL. Not much.

LOUISE. We missed our chance——

KARL. Don't talk like that, it sounds so depressing——

(*They turn away from each other.*)

LOUISE. What's the name of your agents in Sydney?

KARL. Eldrich, Lincoln and Barret.

LOUISE (*going over to kiss him*). Give them my love.

(*She pats his face very gently and sweetly and goes quickly away off up* R. *He makes a movement as if to follow her, then pauses and lights a cigarette. He hums for a moment the tune to which they were dancing and then goes up to the rail where he stands leaning against a post looking out into the morning.* GEORGE DAVIES *and* EVA BLAKE *come quietly, almost furtively on from* L. *They talk in whispers.*)

EVA (L. *of* L. *table*). It's awfully light.

GEORGE (*coming down* C.). There's nobody about.

EVA. Oh, George, you're so wonderful.

GEORGE. Shhh!

(*They kiss swiftly.*)

I suppose it's all right about the Baileys?

EVA. Yes, Marion promised—she'll never say a word.

GEORGE. I won't take you right up to the house, I'll just drop you off at the end of the garden—— (*Moving* R.)

EVA. Oh, George, you think of everything——

KARL. Oh, excuse me? Is your name Eva?

EVA. Yes.

KARL. I congratulate you.

(*They go out up* R. KARL *comes down and kicks* IPPAGA *gently.*)

KARL. Wake up—wake up, it's morning——

IPPAGA *stretches himself as*

The CURTAIN *falls.*

PROPERTY PLOT

As used at the Phœnix Theatre

On Side Table.
  Laid out periodicals.
  Tin high vase of red flowers.

On Balustrade.
  Two pots of exotic red flowers.

On Table L.
  2 empty sherry glasses.
  Ashtray, with ashes in.

On Table R.
  Ashtray.

Off L.
  Tray with 4 glasses of whisky.
    ,,   ,, ,,   ,,   ,,   ,,

Off R.
  Tray of 2 empty glasses.

Scene II.

 Bring on:
  Plate of 3 sandwiches for table R.
  Wooden tray of 4 dirty plates, knives and forks for table L.
  Slide box.

Off stage.
  Piano.
  4 chairs and music-stands.

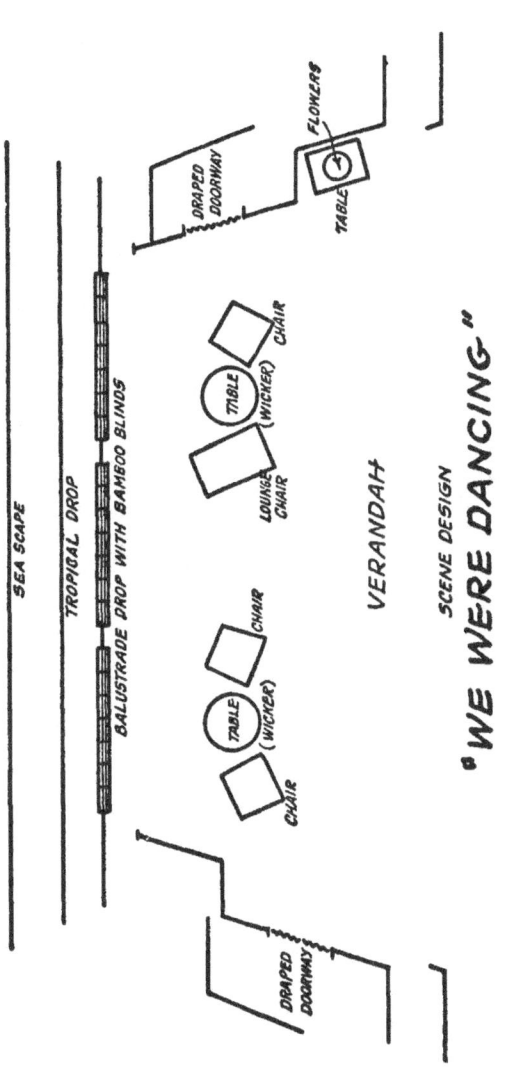

OTHER TITLES AVAILABLE FROM SAMUEL FRENCH

OUTRAGE
Itamar Moses

Drama / 8m, 2f / Unit Set

In Ancient Greece, Socrates is accused of corrupting the young with his practice of questioning commonly held beliefs. In Renaissance Italy, a simple miller named Menocchio runs afoul of the Inquisition when he develops his own theory of the cosmos. In Nazi Germany, the playwright Bertolt Brecht is persecuted for work that challenges authority. And in present day New England, a graduate student finds himself in the center of a power struggle over the future of the University. An irreverent epic that spans thousands of years, *Outrage* explores the power of martyrdom, the power of theatre, and how the revolutionary of one era become the tyrant of the next.

SAMUELFRENCH.COM

OTHER TITLES AVAILABLE FROM SAMUEL FRENCH

THE DECORATOR
Donald Churchill

Comedy / 1m, 2f / Interior

Marcia returns to her flat to find it has not been painted as she arranged. A part time painter who is filling in for an ill colleague is just beginning the work when the wife of the man with whom Marcia is having an affair arrives to tell all to Marcia's husband. Marcia hires the painter, a part-time actor, to impersonate her husband at the confrontation. Hilarity is piled upon hilarity as the painter, who takes his acting very seriously, portrays the absent husband. The wronged wife decides that the best revenge is to sleep with Marcia's husband, an ecstatic experience for them both. When Marcia learns that the painter/actor has slept with her rival, she demands the opportunity to show him what really good sex is.

"Irresistible."
– *London Daily Telegraph*

"This play will leave you rolling in the aisles....
I all but fell from my seat laughing."
– *London Star*

SAMUELFRENCH.COM

OTHER TITLES AVAILABLE FROM SAMUEL FRENCH

THREE YEARS FROM "THIRTY"
Mike O'Malley

Dramatic Comedy / 4m, 3f / Unit set

This funny, poignant story of a group of 27-year-olds who have known each other since college sold out during its limited run at New York City's Sanford Meisner Theater. Jessica Titus, a frustrated actress living in Boston, has become distraught over local job opportunities and she is feeling trapped in her long standing relationship with her boyfriend Tom. She suddenly decides to pursue her dreams in New York City. Unbeknownst to her, Tom plans to propose on the evening she has chosen to leave him. The ensuing conflict ripples through their lives and the lives of their roommates and friends, leaving all of them to reconsider their careers, the paths of their souls and the questions, demands and definition of commitment.

SAMUELFRENCH.COM

www.ingramcontent.com/pod-product-compliance
Lightning Source LLC
Chambersburg PA
CBHW050303010526
44108CB00040B/2271